W9-BSQ-167

LIGHTNING BOLT BOOKS™

How Do Jets Work?

Buffy Silverman

Lerner Publications Company
Minneapolis

Lerner Publications Company
A division of Lerner Publishing Group, Inc.
241 First Avenue North
Minneapolis, MN 55401 U.S.A.

Website address: www.lernerbooks.com

Library of Congress Cataloging-in-Publication Data

Silverman, Buffy.
   How do jets work? / Buffy Silverman.
       p.   cm. — (Lightning bolt books™—How flight works)
   Includes index.
   ISBN 978-0-7613-8967-5 (lib. bdg. : alk. paper)
   1. Airplanes—Piloting—Juvenile literature. 2. Jet planes—Juvenile literature. I. Title.
TL710.S487 2013
629.132—dc23   2012013839

Manufactured in the United States of America
1 — MG — 12/31/12

Table of Contents

On the Runway

A jet backs out of the gate. The pilot and the copilot sit in the cockpit. They can't see behind the plane to steer it. So a tractor must push it.

Tractors help jets leave the gate.

Workers unhook the tractor. The pilot starts the engines and steers the plane.

This plane is facing forward. Now the pilot can steer it.

A line of planes waits on the runway. The pilots listen for instructions from the control tower.

People in the control tower direct plane traffic. They watch planes near and far. They tell pilots when to take off and land.

This is a control tower.

Time for Takeoff

The control tower told the pilot of this plane to take off. The plane speeds down the runway. Under its wings are two jet engines. The engines move the plane forward.

A fan pulls air into the front of each engine. The air is squeezed into a narrow space and heats up. Fuel is sprayed onto the hot air. The fuel burns.

This is a fan on a jet engine.

Hot gases shoot out of the back of the engines. That makes the plane zoom forward.

Hot gases make this plane move. The force that moves a plane forward is called thrust.

The pilot pushes the throttle. The throttle sends more fuel to the engines. The plane moves faster.

This is a throttle.

Air rubs against a plane as it moves. It slows the plane.

Moving air that slows a plane is called drag.

Going Up!

The plane starts to rise. What makes it go up? The shape of the wings gives it lift. Lift pushes things up.

A wing is rounded on top. The bottom is flat. Air flows over and under the wings. It flows faster over the rounded top. The faster air presses less on the wing.

Do you see this wing's rounded top?

The air under the wings moves slower.

It pushes the plane up.

15

Wing flaps help a plane take off too. A pilot tilts the flaps down. This changes the shape so the wings have more lift.

Wing flaps are down during takeoff.

Large jet planes need huge wings. The wings lift the weight of the plane.

Weight pulls things down. Air pushing up under the wings lifts the plane off the ground.

The plane rises higher. The pilot raises the wheels and pulls in the wing flaps. Now there is less drag slowing the plane. The pilot turns the plane by moving flaps on the tail and ends of the wings.

The wheels and the wing flaps go up as a plane flies higher.

The plane speeds faster and faster. Its wings lift it higher and higher.

The faster a plane goes, the more lift it has.

Above the Clouds

Soon a jet reaches its cruising altitude. That's the height where a plane stays for most of the flight.

Jets often cruise between 28,000 and 35,000 feet (8,534 to 10,668 meters).

Jets going from east to west fly at certain heights. Jets flying from west to east fly at different heights. This keeps the planes from crashing into one another.

Planes going in different directions fly at different heights.

A jet plane flies above rain clouds. Jets move up or down to avoid rough air.

Flight attendants keep passengers safe. They tell passengers when to buckle their seat belts. They tell them when they can walk around the cabin.

This is a flight attendant. The inside of the plane is called the cabin. That's where flight attendants work.

Landing

It's time for the plane to land. The pilot pulls back the throttle. Less fuel flows to the engines. The plane slows.

The plane starts to descend. That means it slowly flies lower and lower. The pilot lowers the wing flaps to slow the plane. The pilot also lowers the landing gear.

Have you ever been near a landing plane? Then you may have seen its landing gear.

The runway is near.

The pilot tilts the plane's nose up.

Wheels hit the ground first.

The nose of the plane drops. The engines are reversed so gases shoot out of the front. The brakes screech. The plane slows. It stops when it reaches the gate.

This plane has landed!

Parts of a Jet

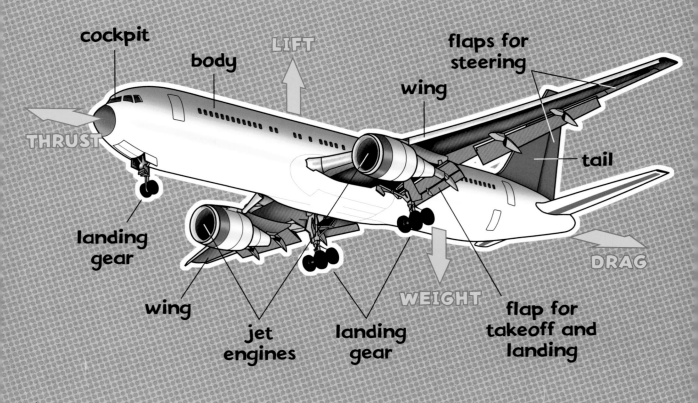

cockpit

body

LIFT

flaps for
steering

wing

THRUST

tail

landing
gear

wing

jet
engines

landing
gear

WEIGHT

DRAG

flap for
takeoff and
landing

Fun Facts

- Jet engines let jets fly superfast. The X-43A flies almost ten times the speed of sound. That's about one hundred times faster than a car on a highway.

- The Airbus A380 is the largest passenger jet. It holds 525 to 853 passengers.

- Cargo jets don't carry passengers. Instead, they carry packages, cars, letters, and horses. Cargo jets even carry other airplanes!

- You can use a balloon to see how a jet engine powers a jet. Blow up the balloon. Pinch it closed. Let the balloon go. Air streams out of one end. The balloon flies in the opposite direction.

Glossary

cockpit: a space in the front of an airplane with instruments used by the pilot and the copilot

control tower: a tower at an airport from which air traffic is controlled

descend: to go from a higher place to a lower place

drag: the force that slows a plane moving through the air

landing gear: the part that supports the weight of an airplane when it is on the ground

lift: a force that lets an airplane rise in the air

pilot: a person who flies a plane. A copilot assists the pilot during a flight.

throttle: equipment that controls the flow of fuel to an engine

wing flap: a hinged part of an airplane wing that is extended when an airplane takes off or lands

Further Reading

Moore, Rob. *Why Do Airplanes Fly?* New York: PowerKids Press, 2010.

NASA: Airplanes
http://www.grc.nasa.gov/WWW/k-12/UEET/StudentSite/airplanes.html

NATCA Kids' Corner
http://www.natca.org/career_day_classroom_materials.aspx#content

Riehle, Mary Ann McCabe. *A Is for Airplane: An Aviation Alphabet.* Chelsea, MI: Sleeping Bear Press, 2009.

Schulz, Walter A. *Johnny Moore and the Wright Brothers' Flying Machine.* Minneapolis: Millbrook Press, 2011.

Index

Photo Acknowledgments

The images in this book are used with the permission of: © Krys Bailey/Alamy, p. 1; Adrian Pingstone/Wikimedia Foundation, Inc., p. 2; © Richard A. Brooks/AFP/Getty Images, p. 4; © Simon Littlejohn/Alamy, p. 5; © Martin Shields/Alamy, p. 6; © Karen Bleier/AFP/Getty Images, p. 7; © John Henley/CORBIS, p. 8; © iStockphoto.com/Terraxplorer, p. 9; © Ramon Berk/Dreamstime.com, p. 10; © Vladimir Maravic/Vetta/Getty Images, p. 11; © Brian Stablyk/Photographer's Choice/Getty Images, p. 12; © Chris Selby/Alamy, p. 13; © Tongho58/Flickr Open/Getty Images, p. 14; © EGimages/Alamy, p. 15; Adrian Pingstone/Wikimedia Foundation, Inc., p. 16; © Christophe Lehenaff/Photononstop/Getty Images, p. 17; © Icholakov/Dreamstime.com, p. 18; © iStockphoto.com/Ilda masa, pp. 19, 31; © Yasuhide Fumoto/Digital Vision/Getty Images, p. 20; © Paul Taylor/Stone/Getty Images, p. 21; © Gabriel Bouys/AFP Creative/Getty Images, p. 22; © Jack Sullivan/Alamy, p. 23; © Inspirestock/Glow Images, p. 24; © Nation Wong/Photographer's Choice/Getty Images, p. 25; © Geraldine Doran/Dreamstime.com, p. 26; © Roc Canals Photography/Flickr/Getty Images, p. 27; © Laura Westlund/Independent Picture Service, p. 28.

Front cover: © iStockphoto.com/luminis.

Main body text set in Johann Light 30/36.